Wyoming

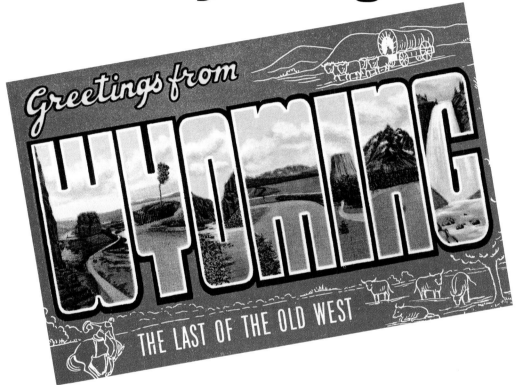

Greetings from WYOMING

THE LAST OF THE OLD WEST

Jim Ollhoff

Visit us at
www.abdopublishing.com

Published by ABDO Publishing Company, 8000 West 78th Street, Suite 310, Edina, Minnesota 55439 USA. Copyright ©2010 by Abdo Consulting Group, Inc. International copyrights reserved in all countries. No part of this book may be reproduced in any form without written permission from the publisher. The Checkerboard Library™ is a trademark and logo of ABDO Publishing Company.

Printed in the United States.

Editor: John Hamilton
Graphic Design: Sue Hamilton
Cover Illustration: Neil Klinepier
Cover Photo: iStock Photo

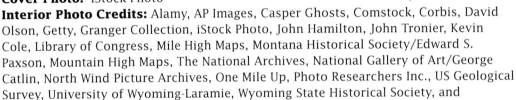

Manufactured with paper containing at least 10% post-consumer waste

Interior Photo Credits: Alamy, AP Images, Casper Ghosts, Comstock, Corbis, David Olson, Getty, Granger Collection, iStock Photo, John Hamilton, John Tronier, Kevin Cole, Library of Congress, Mile High Maps, Montana Historical Society/Edward S. Paxson, Mountain High Maps, The National Archives, National Gallery of Art/George Catlin, North Wind Picture Archives, One Mile Up, Photo Researchers Inc., US Geological Survey, University of Wyoming-Laramie, Wyoming State Historical Society, and Yellowstone National Park-Jim Peaco and Doug Smith.
Statistics: State population statistics taken from 2008 U.S. Census Bureau estimates. City and town population statistics taken from July 1, 2007, U.S. Census Bureau estimates. Land and water area statistics taken from 2000 Census, U.S. Census Bureau.

Library of Congress Cataloging-in-Publication Data

Ollhoff, Jim, 1959-
  Wyoming / Jim Ollhoff.
      p. cm. -- (The United States)
  Includes index.
  ISBN 978-1-60453-687-4
  1. Wyoming--Juvenile literature. I. Title.

  F761.3.O45 2010
  978.7--dc22
                                2008053098

Table of Contents

The Equality State

Wyoming is the 10th-largest state, but it is the state with the fewest people. This makes for wide-open spaces, and lots of land for cattle to graze. It is a rugged, but beautiful land.

Thousands of people crossed Wyoming in the 1800s. Wyoming became a highway to the West. Today, near Guernsey, Wyoming, people can still see the ruts of the wagon train wheels ground into the soft sandstone rock.

The Pony Express was the first mail service to the West. Its riders crossed Wyoming in the early 1860s. After that, the Transcontinental Railroad came through, connecting the East Coast and the West Coast.

Known as "The Equality State," Wyoming in 1869 was the first state to grant women the right to vote.

Wyoming's Grand Teton National Park is famous for its beautiful mountains, lakes, flowers, and wildlife.

Quick Facts

Name: Taken from a Munsee Native American word that means, "at the big plains," or "on the great plain."

State Capital: Cheyenne

Date of Statehood: July 10, 1890 (44th state)

Population: 532,668 (50th-most populous state)

Area (Total Land and Water): 97,818 square miles (253,347 sq km), 10th-largest state

Largest City: Cheyenne, population 55,641

Nicknames: Equality State, Big Wyoming, Cowboy State

Motto: Equal Rights

State Bird: Meadowlark

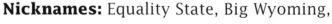
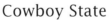

Gannett Peak

Belle Fourche River

State Flower: Indian Paintbrush

State Gemstone: Jade

State Tree: Plains Cottonwood

State Song: "Wyoming"

Highest Point: Gannett Peak, 13,804 feet (4,207 m)

Lowest Point: Belle Fourche River, 3,099 feet (945 m)

Average July Temperature: 67°F (19°C)

Record High Temperature: 115°F (46°C), August 8, 1983, in Basin

Average January Temperature: 19°F (-7°C)

Record Low Temperature: -66°F (-54°C), February 9, 1933, at Moran

Average Annual Precipitation: 13 inches (33 cm)

Number of U.S. Senators: 2

Number of U.S. Representatives: 1

U.S. Postal Service Abbreviation: WY

Geography

Yellowstone River is in northwest Wyoming.

Wyoming is a square-shaped state. Utah and Colorado are to the south. To the west sits Utah, Idaho, and Montana. To the north is Montana. On the east side of Wyoming are South Dakota and Nebraska.

In Wyoming, the plains of the Midwest meet the Rocky Mountains. Much of the eastern side of the state is flat, rolling plains. The west side of the state is mountainous. Major rivers include the Snake River, Powder River, Green River, and Yellowstone River.

About half of the land in Wyoming is federal land. This means that the federal government owns it. The Bureau of Land Management supervises the activities that happen on much of Wyoming's federal land.

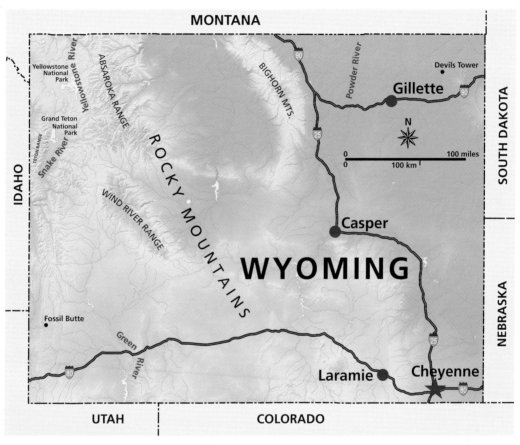

MONTANA

Yellowstone National Park

Yellowstone River

ABSAROKA RANGE

BIGHORN MTS.

Powder River

Devils Tower

Gillette

90

25

N

0   100 miles
0   100 km

IDAHO

SOUTH DAKOTA

Grand Teton National Park

TETON RANGE

Snake River

R O C K Y   M O U N T A I N S

WIND RIVER RANGE

Casper

WYOMING

NEBRASKA

Fossil Butte

Green River

80

25

Laramie

Cheyenne

80

UTAH

COLORADO

Wyoming's total land and water area is 97,818 square miles (253,347 sq km). It is the 10th-largest state. The state capital is Cheyenne.

Much of Wyoming is ranchland for cattle and sheep. The eastern side of the state has a number of farms. The soil is good for growing wheat.

One of the most famous national parks in the United States is Yellowstone National Park. It is the oldest of all the national parks, dating back to 1872. It sits mostly in Wyoming, although a sliver of the park is in Idaho and Montana. Yellowstone is a huge park, with 3,472 square miles (8,992 sq km). It includes the world's most famous geyser, Old Faithful. This geyser is unique because it erupts on a regular basis, about once an hour, shooting water nearly 150 feet (46 m) high.

Old Faithful geyser erupts.

The other national park in Wyoming is Grand Teton National Park. There are two national monuments, Devils Tower and Fossil Butte. There are also a number of national historic trails and wildlife refuges.

The Cathedral Group of mountains in Grand Teton National Park.

Climate and Weather

A state's weather is often affected by its elevation. In the United States, only Colorado has a higher elevation than Wyoming. This high elevation makes the climate a little cooler than the surrounding states. Summer temperatures rarely get higher than 100 degrees Fahrenheit (38°C).

Much of Wyoming tends to be arid, which means it gets very little rain. The western half of the state often sees only 4-8 inches (10-20 cm) of rain per year. However, Wyoming's mountains affect how much rain falls. Some areas receive 45 inches (114 cm) of rain and snow each year.

Much of the land in Wyoming is very dry.

Wyoming can have severe weather. Hail is common. Thunderstorms come most often in late spring and early summer. Tornadoes tend to be small and quick. They are seen most often in the southeast corner of the state.

Lightning strikes a mountain near Jackson Hole, Wyoming.

Plants and Animals

Because there are so few people in Wyoming, it is a great place for animals. Buffalo, or bison, can be found all over the state. It is the official state mammal of Wyoming.

Elk and pronghorn antelope are also common. There are more pronghorn in Wyoming than any other state. Moose and bighorn sheep are other big animals that can be found in Wyoming, especially in the northern parts of the state.

Bears are found mostly in Yellowstone National Park. Coyotes and bobcats love Wyoming's wide-open spaces.

Wild horses live in the open ranges of Wyoming. They are descended from the horses brought to this country by the Spanish in the 1500s. Most of the wild horse herds live in the southwest part of the state.

Two bull moose fight to win a mate.

Black Bear

Coyote

Pronghorn

Pheasant

Grouse, quail, partridge, and pheasants are found throughout Wyoming. Ducks, geese, wild turkeys, and swans are found all over, as well. Bald eagles can be found in western Wyoming.

Most of Wyoming is covered with grasses and shrubs. In mountain areas, there are forests. The forests are mostly made up of ponderosa pine, Douglas fir, and Engelmann spruce. Lodgepole pine is common in the north and south.

Cutthroat Trout

Wyoming has more than 20 species of game fish, including many kinds of trout, bass, crappie, bluegill, and walleye. In fact, the world record for a California golden trout was 28 inches (71 cm) long, caught in Cook Lake in 1948.

Bison are Wyoming's state mammal.

History

There were many Native American tribes in Wyoming before the Europeans came. These tribes included the Cheyenne, Sioux, Arapaho, Blackfeet, Nez Percé, and Shoshone.

French trappers may have hunted and explored the area in the 1700s. Men of Europe liked to wear hats made of beaver fur. For years,

A beaver fur top hat.

trappers entered Wyoming to trap and trade beaver fur.

The first known white person to enter the area was John Colter. He had been a member of the Lewis and Clark Expedition (1804-1806). Colter came to Wyoming in 1807. He was one of the first white explorers to enter the Yellowstone area.

John Colter is sometimes considered to be the first mountain man. Mountain men traveled great distances, hunting and living off the land.

Mountain man John Colter stands with York. Both were members of the Lewis and Clark Expedition. Later, Colter explored the Yellowstone area.

Fur traders established Fort Laramie in 1834. Jim Bridger, another famous mountain man, established Fort Bridger in 1843. Bridger explored the area, and in 1850 discovered a better way through the mountains. Today this is known as Bridger Pass. It was used by the Transcontinental Railroad.

Mountain man Jim Bridger.

In the 1840s and 1850s, about 400,000 people crossed Wyoming to get to the Western states. In the late 1860s, the railroads were built. Cities sprang up to support the railroads, including Cheyenne, Laramie, Rawlins, and Evanston.

In 1868, Wyoming Territory was organized. The first territorial governor was John Campbell. The state constitution was approved in late 1889. The U.S. government admitted Wyoming into the Union in 1890, as the 44th state. Francis Warren served as the first state governor.

Francis Warren served as Wyoming's first governor. He later served as the state's second United States senator.

During World War I, Wyoming became a major supplier of horses for the war effort.

Wyoming was home to a prisoner-of-war camp for captured enemy soldiers during World War II.

Wyoming also housed another kind of camp. It was a relocation camp for Americans who had Japanese ancestry. After Japan bombed Pearl Harbor in 1941, some Americans were concerned about the loyalty of Japanese people living in this country. Were these Japanese-Americans spies? Might they attack the United States?

During World War II, many Japanese-Americans were sent to Heart Mountain Relocation Center.

The U.S. government rounded up thousands of Americans with Japanese ancestors. Some of these Japanese-Americans had been living in America for several generations. It didn't matter. They had to go. Wyoming's Heart Mountain Relocation Center housed almost 11,000 Japanese-Americans.

A family sent to Heart Mountain Relocation Center.

Mining continued to be important after the war. Huge amounts of coal, natural gas, and oil were mined. In 1951, uranium was discovered. For many years, Wyoming was among the top uranium producers in the world.

In the last decades of the 1900s, tourism grew in importance. Mining, agriculture, and tourism continue to be strong industries for Wyoming.

Did You Know?

Wyoming is known as the "Equality State." This is because of the rights that women have had in the state. Historically, women were not allowed to vote in the United States. It wasn't until 1920 that the U.S. Constitution was changed to allow women that right.

However, from its beginning, Wyoming's constitution allowed women the right to vote. Women could cast ballots and hold public office. Wyoming was the first state to pass a law granting women these rights.

Esther Hobart Morris

In 1870, Esther Hobart Morris of South Pass City became the first woman in the United States to be appointed justice of the peace.

In 1894, Estelle Meyer became the superintendent of public instruction in Wyoming. She was the first woman elected to state office in the United States.

The first woman governor of any U.S. state was also in Wyoming. Nellie Tayloe Ross of Cheyenne, Wyoming, was elected in 1924.

In 1924, Wyoming's Nellie Tayloe Ross was the first woman elected governor of any state. She took office in January 1925.

People

Chief Washakie (1808?–1900) was a famous warrior, friend to white people, and leader of the Shoshone tribe. Many of Washakie's family were killed by tribal warfare when he was young.

Because he was wise and good in battle, he became chief of the Shoshone tribe. He was also a friend of the white settlers. He kept this friendship even though the U.S. government plundered Shoshone land, and broke treaties they made with the tribe. Washakie always sought the best for his people, and was commended for his treatment of white settlers. He was buried at Wyoming's Fort Washakie with full military honors.

Dick Cheney (1941-) served as vice president of the United States from 2001-2009. He was born in Nebraska, but grew up in Casper, Wyoming. He graduated from the University of Wyoming, earning degrees in political science. Cheney worked as an intern in the Richard Nixon administration, and held several different jobs, until becoming White House chief of staff for President Gerald Ford. Cheney was then elected to the U.S. House of Representatives for Wyoming, serving from 1979-1989. His next job was as secretary of defense for President George H.W. Bush. In 2001, he became vice president, serving two terms with President George W. Bush.

Nellie Tayloe Ross (1876-1977) was America's first female governor. She was born in Missouri, and went to school in Nebraska. In 1902, she married William Ross. He decided to practice law in the West, so they moved to Cheyenne, Wyoming.

William Ross became governor of Wyoming in 1922, but died in 1924. Nellie was elected to succeed her husband. She became Wyoming's governor in January 1925.

In 1933, President Franklin Roosevelt asked Ross to be the director of the U.S. Mint. The mint produces gold and silver coins in the United States. Ross was the first woman to hold this job, and kept it until she retired in 1953. Ross lived to the age of 101, traveling, writing, and helping people her entire life.

Buffalo Bill Cody (1846-1917) was a scout, frontiersman, and showman. William Cody was born in Iowa, and later moved to Kansas. He worked many jobs to help his family, including trapping and gold mining. He was a rider for the Pony Express, and a soldier during the Civil War.

When train tracks were laid across the United States, he hunted food for the workers on the railroad. He killed buffalo, earning the nickname "Buffalo Bill." He also worked as a scout for the U.S. Army.

He began Buffalo Bill's Wild West show in the 1870s. He used his popularity to help develop Wyoming. Today, the Buffalo Bill Historical Center is in Cody, Wyoming.

Cities

Cheyenne is the largest city in Wyoming, and its capital. The city began in 1867 when the Union Pacific Railroad was built in the area. The city was named after the area's Native American tribe, the Cheyenne. Settlers came quickly to the new city. Today, Cheyenne has a population of 55,641. It holds many festivals and community events. Some of the most popular are Cheyenne Frontier Days, Oktoberfest, the Christmas Parade, and the Goblin Walk.

Casper began as a trading post for settlers traveling on the Oregon Trail in 1840s and 1850s. Later, it became a military post for the U.S. Army. The city is named after Lieutenant Caspar Collins. The young man died trying to protect a wagon train from Lakota  warriors. A misspelling caused the name change to "Casper" when the city was established in 1888. Casper served as a stopping point for the railroad. Ranchers and settlers moved in. In 1890, oil was discovered in the area. Casper became a center for oil refining. Coal and uranium mining are also important. Casper's population is 53,003.

Laramie in 1908.

Laramie is in the southeast section of the state. Its population is 27,241. When railroads were built in the area in 1868, the town followed. At first, Laramie was without any lawmen. It was a wild place. The town grew and developed. In 1886, Laramie became home to the University of Wyoming. Today, tourists are drawn to Laramie's many outdoor activities. Skiing, mountain biking, hiking, and fishing are popular sports in and around the town.

Gillette has a population of 25,031. Established in 1892, it is located in the northeast part of the state. Huge deposits of coal and oil are located in the area. Residents of Gillette call it "the energy capital of the nation."

Transportation

The main east-west interstate is I-80. It roughly follows the route of the first Transcontinental Railroad. I-80 goes through Cheyenne, Laramie, and Evanston. I-25 goes north and south, through Casper and Cheyenne. I-90, in the northeast corner of the state, passes through Gillette and Sheridan.

An I-80 tunnel burrows under a bluff near Green River.

There are no passenger trains in Wyoming. However, many railroads still carry loads of freight.

There are nine commercial airports in Wyoming, and more than 30 smaller airfields. Jackson Hole Airport is located in Grand Teton National Park. It is the only airport in a United States national park. This unusual airport's main building looks like a pioneer's log cabin.

Jackson Hole Airport is the only airport in the United States located within a national park. The Grand Teton mountains rise up behind the airstrip.

Natural Resources

About half of Wyoming's land is used for agriculture. Most is grazing land for sheep and cattle. The state has more than 11,000 farms. Wheat, oats, barley, corn, sugar beets, and potatoes are some of the main crops grown in Wyoming.

Ranchers in Wyoming take their cattle up in the mountains to summer pastures.

Wyoming is rich in minerals. Oil and natural gas are found in the northeast. Wyoming is the largest producer of coal in the United States. About one-third of the nation's uranium is found in Wyoming. Limestone, gypsum, and iron ore are mined in the state.

Wyoming has the largest known supply of trona in the world. Trona is a mineral used in paper, soaps, baking soda, water softeners, and medicines.

Trona.

Industry

Mining, agriculture, and tourism are the three main industries in Wyoming.

A large crane is used to dig for uranium at a mining site near Casper, Wyoming.

Mining includes oil, coal, uranium, natural gas, and trona. As energy prices change, the economy of Wyoming changes as well.

Agriculture in the state is mostly ranching, primarily beef and sheep. More than 91 percent of the land in Wyoming is rural. Wyoming's agricultural products are valued at more than $1.1 billion.

Wyoming's tourist industry is growing. Tourism accounts for about 10 percent of the jobs in the state. Wyoming's two national parks are Yellowstone and Grand Teton. There are a number of national monuments and national forests. More than six million people visit these federal lands each year.

Devils Tower National Monument is a popular tourist attraction. Many people come to climb the 867-foot (264-m) -tall rock tower.

Sports

Wyoming has no professional major league sports teams. However, the Casper Ghosts are a minor league baseball team. They are associated with the Colorado Rockies, a professional major league baseball team.

The University of Wyoming in Laramie has many sports teams. The Cowboys and Cowgirls play football, basketball, soccer, volleyball, swimming, track, wrestling, and many other sports. They even have a successful rugby team.

The University of Wyoming's Cowboys and Cowgirls are popular teams.

Wyoming's open spaces and limited population make it an excellent place for a wide variety of outdoor activities. Tourists enjoy visiting dude ranches and trail riding.

Both residents and visitors like to hike, backpack, fish, and watch birds. The adventurous enjoy whitewater rafting, parasailing, hang gliding, and exploring the state's caves.

The adventurous enjoy whitewater rafting on the Snake River in Grand Teton National Park.

Entertainment

The Old West is still a part of life in Wyoming. Residents are proud of their Western traditions and culture. The world's largest rodeo is held in Cheyenne, Wyoming. A number of other rodeos are held all over the state. Cheyenne's Frontier Days has been celebrated every year since 1897. This festival has everything from country music to bull riding.

Bull riding during Frontier Days.

Several of Wyoming's larger cities have orchestras and music festivals. Cheyenne and Casper have symphony orchestras. There is a chamber music festival in Laramie each year.

Wyoming has a number of museums. Many explore the history of the heroes and villains of the Old West. A number of the state's festivals celebrate the cowboy heritage. There are even gatherings where people share their cowboy poetry.

An actor portrays Buffalo Bill Cody in Old Trail Town, an outdoor museum of historic Old West buildings in Cody, Wyoming.

Timeline

Pre-1800s—Cheyenne, Sioux, Arapaho, Blackfeet, Nez Percé, Shoshone, and other tribes inhabit Wyoming.

1807—John Colter explores Wyoming and the Yellowstone area.

1834—Fur traders establish Fort Laramie.

1843—Fort Bridger is established.

1840s-1850s—Wyoming becomes a crossroads for people going west.

1860s—Railroads are built.

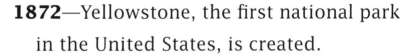

1872—Yellowstone, the first national park in the United States, is created.

1890—Wyoming becomes the 44th state.

1925—Nellie Tayloe Ross is sworn in as Wyoming's governor. She becomes the nation's first female governor.

1941-1945—Prisoner-of-war camps and Japanese-American relocation centers are set up in Wyoming during World War II.

1951—Uranium is discovered in Wyoming.

2009—Wyoming resident Dick Cheney retires from politics after serving two terms as vice president of the U.S.

Glossary

Arapaho—A Native American tribe who lived on the plains of Wyoming and Colorado.

Arid—A climate that has very little rain or snow.

Blackfeet—A Native American tribe that lived on the plains. They often used ashes to stain their moccasins black.

Cheyenne—A Great Plains Native American tribe. The capital of Wyoming is named after the Cheyenne.

Elevation—The height of a given location based on how far from sea level it is.

Geyser—A spring that shoots up hot water with explosive force from time to time. Old Faithful is among several famous geysers found in Wyoming's Yellowstone National Park.

Mountain Men—Hunters, guides, and explorers who traveled in the wilds of Wyoming and lived off the land.

Nez Percé—A Native American tribe who lived in the mountain valleys of Wyoming, and who traveled seasonally to other areas.

Pony Express—A way of delivering mail from 1860-1861. A relay of riders delivered letters from Missouri to California.

Shoshone—A Native American tribe that lived in western Wyoming. Sacagawea was probably a Shoshone tribe member.

Sioux—An alliance of Great Plains Native American tribes who spoke three related languages: Dakota, Nakota, and Lakota.

Transcontinental Railroad—The first railroad that stretched across the United States from the east to the west. It traveled across Wyoming.

World War I—A war that was fought in Europe from 1914 to 1918, involving countries around the world. The United States entered the war in April 1917.

World War II—A conflict across the world, lasting from 1939-1945. The United States entered the war in December 1941.

Index